Acknowledgments

The idea of publishing a children's book about Amarillo and the Panhandle area came from the Amarillo Public Library staff in 1994 and was accomplished with the help of the Junior League of Amarillo. Through the efforts of the Picture Book Task Force, Amarillo: The Yellow Rose of Texas became a reality. The Picture Book Task Force is pleased that this children's book has been written, illustrated, and published by Texans. Volunteers on the Junior League Picture Book Task Force include:

Edie Carter, Coordinator
Nancy Beasley / Susan Hoyl
Diantha Steinhilper

In addition, valuable expertise and assistance were provided by Amarillo Public Library employees. Library staff members who served on the Picture Book Task Force were:

Luke Morrison / Pat Mullin

The Picture Book Task Force expresses its sincere appreciation to Ed Eakin and his staff for believing in the project; to Arvis Stewart for his creative artistry and generosity; to Sarah Williamson for her research and for creating Prairie Dog Pete and his tale; and to the membership of the Junior League of Amarillo for its emotional and financial support.

Special thanks is also offered to these friends in our community for their assistance with the publication of this work:

Jo Baker / Carol Kritselis
Luskey's Western Store
Panhandle Plains Historical Museum

Amarillo
The Yellow Rose of Texas

Written by
Sarah Heinze Williamson

Illustrations by
Arvis L. Stewart

A special project of
The Junior League of Amarillo

EAKIN PRESS ★ Austin, Texas

Howdy there, folks, city slickers, and cowpokes,
I'm a very friendly fellow!
The High Plains are my home, and I love to roam
Where it's broad, flat, and yellow.

I live on the prairie, way down in a hole,
And Prairie Dog Pete is my name.
I live here in Texas, the Lone Star State,
The state of great wonder and fame!

So get off your feet, come out of the heat
And fluff up a big, cozy pillow —
'Cause I'm here to tell you 'bout the Yellow Rose of Texas,
The city of Amarillo!

Before there were Indians, cowboys, or settlers,
This land was a great shallow sea
Inhabited by dinosaurs and exotic animals
Very strange and different from me!

Then the earth buckled, the water dried,
And the dinosaurs became extinct.
The Caprock was formed, a strata of rock,
An escarpment old and distinct.

At Alibates National Monument–
A place of flint and stones,
Keep in mind that you may find
Ancient weapons, tools, and bones!

In time came the Indians hunting for food
From Asia across the Strait.
That was thousands and thousands of years ago;
No one knows for sure the date.

The Indians hunted mammoths and mastodons
With arrow-pointed spears.
Then they hunted bison, antelope, and deer,
With bow and arrow for years.

Some Indians preferred to wander and hunt,
While others settled down.
They grew maize and squash, cotton and beans,
And pumpkins in the ground.

Then, in 1541,
A Spaniard named Coronado
Came to explore — a conquistador —
And called the plains Llano Estacado.

Coronado explored along the floor
Of a canyon he named Palo Duro.
He seemed very bold, but finding no gold,
He chose not to stay, but to go.

Before he departed, he offered his thanks
For provisions of water and game.
He felt bereft, but to us he left
A few Spanish names and his fame.

In the late 1600s, from across the border,
Came the Mexican *cibolero*.
He searched far and wide for buffalo hides
Then returned to his *rancho* in Mexico.

A century later came a new kind of trader,
The shrewd New Mexican *Comanchero*.
He traded with Apaches, and then Comanches,
And wore a big *sombrero*.

The Kwahadi Comanches were ruled by a chief;
Quanah Parker was his name.
He became a great warrior and led his native
    people,
The Comanches — Lords of the Plains.

Indian, Spanish, French, and Mexican,
All had once been here.
But the United States claimed Texas its state —
1845 was the year.

A very old route, the Santa Fe Trail,
Brought travelers across the plain.
They braved blizzards and sand and Indian bands
And prayed for the sky to send rain.

Over the years, overcoming their fears,
The pioneers came to Texas.
They had hopes, dreams, and money-making
  schemes,
But the land contained many vexes.

With cattle in tow, down to Palo Duro
Charles Goodnight came a ropin' —
Sittin' high in the saddle, herding 1,600 cattle.
The Llano was wide, vast, and open.

Soon, barbed wire fences divided the prairie,
Defining the ranching frontier.
During roundup, cowboys branded the Hereford
   and Angus
In the spring and fall of the year.

To keep all those cattle from dying of thirst,
The ranches required fresh water.
So wells were drilled for pumping windmills
To tap the Ogallala Aquifer.

On the heels of the ranchers followed the farmers —
They, too, were seeking land.
They would look at the sky and say, "My, oh, my,"
For little water was at hand.

They drilled deep wells and erected windmills,
But theirs was no life of ease.
In the north, they grew wheat; in the south, cotton.
They even had to plant their own trees!

As large herds of cattle ate more prairie grass,
The farmers realized a need.
So they planted sorghum, hay, and alfalfa,
Providing the ranchers with feed.

As ranching and farming brought promise of
   wealth,
Settlers poured onto the plains.
To transport goods, crops, cattle, and people,
Along came steam-powered trains!

A townsite was formed from which to ship cattle —
The settlers called it Amarillo.
Nearby were yellow flowers and Amarillo Creek —
Amarillo is Spanish for "yellow."

As settlers spread the word, a good thing occurred;
I guess you'd call it fate:
Men and women with hope and ability to cope
Migrated to Texas, our state!

In 1918, beneath a Panhandle ranch,
An era in history unfurled:
A pioneer drilled, hitting a huge gas field —
The largest, at that time, in the world.

To his great pleasure, he discovered more treasure,
For he also hit "black gold":
Oil had formed where plants and animals swarmed
In the shallow sea of old!

Pipelines were laid, through which oil and gas
    flowed,
To cities of the U. S. A.
Cars are fueled and homes heated when cool
By oil and gas products today!

In the 1930s, we experienced worries
That never before had been faced.
The Great Depression, a time of recession,
Nearly laid our country to waste.

For lack of rain, cattle died on the plain,
And all the fields were in blight.
Dust rose in the wind and clouds failed to send
Rain to lessen our plight.

The lack of jobs caused hunger and despair
And soon got everyone down.
But we shouldered together and worked hard to
    weather
Hard times that had hit our town.

During World War II, our patriotism grew,
As many needs in our nation arose.
Our citizens helped to form the national defense
Protecting us from our foes.

From our huge gas field, we used helium to fill
Navy convoy-guiding blimps.
They protected ships at sea, by warning them to flee
Enemy subs that they would glimpse.

In medicine, oceanography, and space exploration,
Helium is a useful gas.
As we sing party tunes, it fills our balloons —
No odor, no flames, low mass!

Today, we have libraries, museums, and
   recreation —
The best High Plains health care, too!
To get an education attend Amarillo College
Or West Texas A&M U.

In Palo Duro Canyon, come to see "TEXAS,"
An outdoor drama performed on a stage.
See Cal Farley's Boys Ranch, which gives a second
   chance,
To children of every age.

Symphony, ballet, opera, art, theater
Altogether our lives enhance.
Two-step, Promenade, and Cotton-Eyed Joe —
We Texans love to dance!

We see beautiful sunsets, vivid moon, bright stars,
Rain, sleet, snow, and hail.
On the prairie live coyotes, prairie dogs, rabbits,
Pheasant, deer, and quail.

Though the wind often blows, everyone knows
In time it stops bending the trees.
Be still, feel its peace — a quiet, gentle breeze —
Barely rippling the prairie grass seas!

On many a night, white light streaks the sky,
Clouds rumble and crash — what a sound!
With dawn on the horizon, see a glorious sun a risin' —
How the moodiness of nature does astound!

To the Indians, Spanish, and fearless pioneers —
Their legacy I salute and I hail!
To the future generation, I encourage determination
In telling the Panhandle tale!

Faith, hope, stubbornness, and true grit
Sustained our forefathers here.
To their great glory I dedicate this story,
Keeping their memory near!

So, adios, folks, city slickers, and cowpokes,
I'm a tired and tuckered-out fellow!
I think I will doze and dream of the Yellow Rose,
My city, my home — *Amarillo!*

Books to Read

Price, B. Byron, and Frederick W. Rathjen. *The Golden Spread*. Northridge, California: Windsor Publications, Inc., 1986.

Robertson, Pauline Durrett, and R. L. Robertson. *Panhandle Pilgrimage*. Amarillo, Texas: Paramount Publishing Company, 1978.